MY LAST

Breaking the Curse to Embrace the Blessing

La'Trae Wilson

D1227398

Copyright © 2020   La'Trae Wilson

Book Package and Publication:
Leadership DevelopME, LLC: www.leadershipdevelopme.com

All rights reserved. No part of this book may be used or reproduced
by any means, graphic, electronic, or mechanical, including photocopying,
recording, taping or by any information storage retrieval system without the
written permission of the publisher except in the case of brief quotations
embodied in critical articles and reviews.

Books may be ordered through booksellers or by contacting:
La'Trae Wilson
Website: www.destined2Bblessed.com

Because of the dynamic nature of the Internet, any web addresses or links
contained in this book may have changed since publication and may no
longer be valid. The views expressed in this work are solely those of the
author and do not necessarily reflect the views of the publisher,
and the publisher hereby disclaims any responsibility for them.

Any people depicted in stock imagery provided by Thinkstock are models,
and such images are being used for illustrative purposes only.

Certain stock imagery © Thinkstock.

**Some names and identifying details have been changed to
protect the privacy of individuals.**

ISBN: 978-1-71661-563-4
Library of Congress Control Number: 2020917088

Scriptures are taken from the KING JAMES VERSION (KJV):
KING JAMES VERSION, public domain.

Printed in the United States of America.
All rights reserved.

DEDICATION

My most profound appreciation goes to Willie & Sylvia Wilson, Jim, Wayne, Del, Tecia & my late sister, Chell, who provided helpful comments and suggestions. To Jaylen, who is my world, you're the reason for my lifestyle change, and to my goddaughters, you all are my hearts, and you all bring me so much joy. To my best friends, Chyonne and Toni, thank you for all your support and friendship for over 20 years. Special thanks also go to my PFBC Church Family, who prayed for me and spoke life into me. I thank you. I would also like to express my gratitude to my family and friends for their moral support and warm encouragement.

I love you all.

TABLE OF CONTENTS

INTRODUCTION

Imagine waking up, getting ready for work, and something just doesn't feel right. So, you brush it off and continue getting ready for work. You arrive at work and the unthinkable happens, your water breaks. Thoughts start racing through your mind "How can this be?" "It's too early, I'm only 24 weeks pregnant, it's not time!"

So, you call your mom and tell her what's going on, and she thinks you're playing because the same thing happened to your sister weeks before. You reassure her that you're not playing, and you need to be rushed to the hospital as soon as possible. On the ride to the hospital, so many thoughts are going through your head, "Will the baby and I be okay?" "Why is this happening to me?" "Why is my mother driving so slowly? You need her to put the pedal to the metal." You finally arrive at the hospital, and they're hooking you up to all types of machines, and all you want to know is, "Is my baby going to be okay?"

The doctors finally come to tell you that the lining of your uterus had become very thin and began to leak fluid and became infected, which caused your water to rupture too early. They let you know that the baby is okay and that they will do everything they can to keep the baby inside for as long as they can and make you as comfortable as possible because you will be in the hospital for a while.

As you lay in your hospital bed resting, a nurse comes in your room and suggests that you have an abortion because your baby will have problems, and why would you want that? You're being selfish and only thinking of yourself. Something in your spirit said, "Don't listen to her and trust God." Twenty minutes later, three doctors come into your room and tell you that this was a special case, you're only 24 weeks pregnant and you need to be at least 25 weeks or more for your baby to even survive. They let you know they have seen this before, and the survival rate was very low, but they will do their best to save your baby.

Night comes, and something is not right. You begin to start cramping, and you call for your nurse, and the nurse tells you that you're okay, nothing's wrong, and then you tell her, no, something doesn't feel right. She finally comes in and tells you that you are in labor. You reply labor? Yes, you are in labor, she says. You reply, labor? I can't be! They end up giving you morphine to stop the labor because it's definitely too soon. However, they explain that if you go into labor again, you will definitely have to deliver the baby.

Now you're scared and praying that this doesn't happen any time soon. 24 hours later, you begin to have contractions again, but this time, the baby's heart rate keeps dropping, so they prepare you for an emergency C-section and next thing you know. you're waking up in the recovery room, wondering where your baby is, and if your baby is okay. You finally get to see him, and your baby is hooked up to all types of machines, and you're told that you can only look at him through the window because they're trying to keep him stabilized, and the next few hours will be critical.

In 2001, this was the day that would change my life forever, but that would not be the end; this was just a small glimpse of my life in this book. I want to share some events in my life over an almost 20-year span that I've been afraid to share or just ashamed to admit. And for the first time in 20 years, I'm free from the things that have been holding me back from being my true self. After all, I was the one who created the chaos that bound me from being true to myself. I decided to write a book for a few reasons. The first reason is to free myself from what was once holding me down. The second reason is to help you to identify the cycles that you may be in, and you don't even know you're in. Lastly is to inform someone that may be going through what I've been through that there is a way out, and you're not alone.

This book is for single parents who have a child or children with differences, someone who wants to change the narrative and break the cycle and generational curses. This is for the person that's been in toxic relationships and doesn't know how to identify the toxicity that they are in. It's for the broken person that has been emotionally abused over and over again. And lastly, it's for the person who has said enough is enough but is still unsure about the next steps and looking for support.

I hope that what I've been through will benefit others that may be or have been in similar situations. I hope this book proves that your life matters, and no matter what you've done or what has been done to you, you don't have to sit and be silent anymore.

CHAPTER 1

LEAVING THE NEST

Moving out of your parent's home can often be difficult, particularly if you're not mentally or financially prepared. I just knew I needed my own place because my home wasn't the same after my mom and dad were divorced. I was in the middle of their chaos, and I had had enough.

I recall receiving a phone call, asking if I was still interested in these apartments that I'd signed up for years earlier, as my name was next on the waiting list. I told them I would take the apartment, and I didn't even know where the place was located until after I said yes. Then the individual informed me that it was in West Oakland. I answered, "West Oakland!" I asked if there was anything in East Oakland, but they told me that it wouldn't be available for a bit. Listen, I didn't want to miss the opportunity to be on my own, so I asked when I could see the place and how soon I could move in? They said that I could move in a couple of weeks if I wanted to, and I could see the apartment in a couple of days.

I was excited. I'd finally got a place of my own, and all I could do was thank God. The first person I called was my mom, and I told her that I'd finally received a call about the apartment that I had applied for years earlier, and the first question she asked was, "Where is it?" I replied, "West Oakland." She replied, "West Oakland? Do they have any in East Oakland? Or was that an option?" I explained that if I didn't take the apartment, I'd have to wait, so she gave me her blessing. Then, I ran into the room to tell my dad. He was happy for me, but he also mentioned that I didn't have to go, and I could stay if I wanted to. I told him that it was time for me to move out and get my own place, and I needed my own space. He agreed and asked where the place was. I told him it was in West Oakland, and he said, "West Oakland?" Is there anything in East Oakland? Then he asked if I was sure I wanted to move out there? I said, "Yes, Daddy, I do." He said, "Well, it's just your decision, be safe and responsible because it's not easy to have your own place. I know you can do it, but if you ever need anything, you can always call." I have all the blessings of my parents; it's time to move.

Weeks before Thanksgiving, I got a chance to look at my place. I couldn't believe that I was moving to the West; this was a game-changer. I grew up in East Oakland, so I didn't care that much about West Oakland. All I knew was if you were from the East, you stay out of the West, but now the West was about to be home.

8th and Campbell was my first place; this area of West Oakland was called the "Lower Bottoms," the real hood, undoubtedly something I wasn't used to and wasn't where I wanted to live, but it was God who blessed me, and I was grateful.

I had a one-bedroom apartment with a washer and a dryer hook-up, but there was no refrigerator or stove, so I had to purchase them. I couldn't afford new ones, so I got some used from Santa Clara Appliances on 51st in East Oakland for $200, the best $200 I'd ever invested. I still needed to buy the furniture, but I had to wait because I couldn't afford that yet, so I got an air mattress, made sure I had my T.V. and my phone, and I was GOOD! I was excited about spending my first night in my apartment.

My first night in my apartment was kind of scary. I've never been on my own like this; I've been used to living in a house. I wasn't used to typical apartment building noises, and all the street noise, too. I think I heard gunshots that night, and that wouldn't be the last one either.

Once you go off on your own, you don't necessarily think of the responsibility that comes with living on your own. You have to be responsible for bill's and pay them on time every month, such as rent, electricity, your phone, your cable, and all the other things you need to survive; you have to be the person who supplies these things. So, what are you supposed to do? I know what I did. I went out and got a second job because there were things I wanted to do and places I wanted to be. There was no one to hold me back, and I could go and come as I pleased because I was grown, so I thought.

Factors that you need to establish before you move into an apartment are, would your neighbors be good, respectful, and clean? How secure is the area where your apartment is located? Can you see yourself staying there for a couple of years? If this isn't the case, you should look somewhere else.

Also, another thing you've got to do is save money to move and then save a couple of extra dollars for emergencies because they do come up. I didn't do that; I spent the money as soon as I received it. I went out to eat instead of cooking at home. Almost every weekend, I went to the club. I was on the guest list, and I never paid to get in, but I had to pay for food or drinks when away. At a moment's notice, I 'd head out of town and waste most if not all of my money on trips to Vegas and L.A. And none of this was planned or budgeted because I didn't have a budget. I never took the time out to make one, nor did I adjust my spending patterns when I didn't have my spot.

You're probably asking yourself, "Why is she telling me this?" I'm telling you this because nobody told me, so it's time to speak up. How else are you going to learn? It's a lost generation out here, inexperienced because their parents felt it was best to learn things on their own or in a hard way. Hey, Ma'am and Sir, please stop! You are setting your child or children up for failure, sit down and have these conversations on what it's like to live on your own and the challenges you've learned to live and survive on your own. Some will listen, and others will go out and figure it out the hard way, but at least you sat them down and had a talk with them.

It's time for parents to break the habit of not communicating with their children about real-life issues. If you sit around and talk about reality shows that you watch together, you can talk about breaking cycles too. We need to change the narrative so that we don't lose a generation that doesn't know what reality is and what isn't reality. It's suitable for your child or children to gain knowledge about your mistakes just as much as they learn about your achievements. Your child or children can look at you in ways they've never looked at you before, and that's a great feeling.

It took months for me to actually get my apartment the way I liked it. I didn't have it all, and it was all right with me. By then, I knew that I had to change the way I spent my money. I figured that I needed to be a little more responsible, so I got a credit card. One of the stupidest things I could ever do! I maxed the credit card out and paid it off gradually; then, I maxed it out again.

By now, I'd created debt at the top of my debt. My car-note was past due, the cable bill was late, I had a 30-day notice on my electricity bill, the phone was about to be cut off! Oh, yeah, and I got a couple of eviction notices. All my bills came to $749 a month, and at the time, I was taking home at least $25,000 a year, which was cool in 1999, and it was good for somebody my age with no children. There's no way I should've been able to afford $749 a month, and I took in at least $2,080 a month. So, after paying my bills, I was expected to have $1,334 leftover, but that wasn't the case. So, one day, I sat down and finally made a budget, I finally said that I wanted to get out of debt and grow up and get my things together because I don't want to stay in this apartment forever.

I ended up getting my credit repaired, stopped going out so much, and became a little more responsible with my spending. I started to feel a bit accomplished because of the things I saw myself doing. I thought I had my life under control, and my lifestyle had changed, but that was just the beginning.

I had been in my place for a year now, and I started to feel myself. I wasn't attending church as much as I used to, I had a boyfriend and an ex-boyfriend I was involved with, I didn't care, and I found myself going downhill from there.

CHAPTER 2

I THOUGHT IT WAS LOVE

Love can mask itself in many ways; it can be sweet, affectionate, friendly, caring, loving, never vanishing, and much more. I just knew that in 1999, I thought I'd discovered love when I was attending Chabot College in Hayward. I had transferred from Alameda College to Chabot because of too many distractions, mostly guys and friends, who weren't serious about school.

I needed to get back on track, so I stopped dating, and I changed my school. My best friend, Shanise, would pick me up for school in the morning, and I would catch a bus or get a ride from a friend's home. I was proud of myself; I didn't want to hang out at the cafeteria just like I'd done at my previous school. This time, I was organized, and I was passing all my classes, and I didn't let anyone get in my path. I even had a job at the campus library. I checked the books in and out, and then I put them away. It was a way for me to do my homework without distractions so that I could chill when I got home.

While I was working in the library, I would see most of the students on campus. They either came to check out books, or they returned books. Some of the students would come to study or kill time, so I got to know quite a few of them.

It was a guy named Dre, who would sometimes come to the library. We 'd talk from time to time, and after a while, we'd joke with each other, and soon the laughs turned into flirting. Dre just wasn't my type, so I didn't take all this attention too seriously. I would play it off or go along with it while he was around.

I remember one day walking with Shanise on campus when I saw Dre. I told Shanise he was the guy who had been flirting with me in the library. She looked, and she was like, "I've got a class with him, he seems to be well-educated, you can talk to him." At first, I felt like he wasn't even tall (I like tall guys), but he was different from the other guys I've dated.

I decided to give him a chance. He asked me for my phone number a few days later. I gave it to him, of course, and we ended up talking the same night. We talked about a lot of things, and we found out that we had so many things in common. I found out that we agreed on a variety of things that were relevant to us at that moment, and the conversation wasn't boring at all. Dre had a lot to say and spoke about all kinds of different matters, and the topics went on for a while and never got boring.

After talking for a minute, Dre asked if we could go to the movies one day. I told him that I needed to check my work schedule, and I was going to get back to him. Everything ended up working out, and we went to the movies that Friday.

We 'd see each other at school and talk to each other and talk with each other a little more after we left school. Dre used to go to the library to study or pretend that he was studying, or sometimes, he just came to see me, but he was really serious about his schooling, and that was good for me also because it made me focus a little bit more on my classes, too.

We started to chill at his house or my place, so you know what that means ... yep! SEX, SEX, SEX. He started telling me that he loved me, so I'd say it back because that's how I felt; he was so different from the other guys I dated. I was used to guys who only had nine-to-five jobs or were about that "street life," so a college guy like Dre was different and exciting. I felt it was a step up from what I was used to, and everything was going well.

One day, Dre called and asked if we could talk because he had something important to say to me. We've been talking for a couple of months, and I was curious about what he had to say. Once we talked a couple of days later, he tells me he's got a five-month-old son! I got angry, and I was shocked and hurt.

We'd been dating for a few months, and he has just now mentioned this. I started thinking about our relationship, beginning to doubt a lot of other things that he'd told me. I asked him what else he hadn't mentioned to me? He claimed that his child's mother and he had broken up and that he was trying his best to take care of his kid, but he was not involved with the mother at all. After I calmed down and listened to him, it seemed to make sense. We were always together or on the phone, and how did he find time for something else? Guess what? I kept talking to him like a fool. Yup, I forgave him, and we continued as though nothing had happened.

These were all red flags, and I missed every single one of them. I didn't hold Dre accountable for lying or his actions behind any of them, and someone who would hide a kid would probably lie again. I can't even be mad at Dre because I allowed this kind of treatment, and I didn't love myself enough to leave. I thought that I was lucky because he still wanted to be with me. I was so afraid of losing him and ending our relationship that I tolerated this type of behavior.

Despite the signs, I still thought he was the one for me, but, after a while, our relationship took a turn for the worse, and we took a break from each other. I got involved with someone else after a while.

This guy was more my speed, 6 ft 4 in, light-skin, beautiful eyes and had a good job. Also, he didn't have any kids, loved going to church, and being around his family. He was caring, and he knew how to treat a woman. He was the perfect gentleman, and anything I wanted to do, we did. Anywhere I wanted to go, we went. If I just mentioned something to Eric, he would surprise me with it. He was just that type of guy.

Eric began to fall for me, and I fell for him, but I wasn't over my ex-boyfriend, Dre. Still, having feelings for Dre didn't deter me, and I continued my relationship with Eric, and things got serious. Eventually, he proposed, and I gladly accepted his proposal. I started having second thoughts, so I sabotaged the relationship, as I was immature and broken from my past relationship.

I ended up calling off the engagement, so I could "think things through," but that wasn't the case. I was scared, to be honest. I was 22 years old and just wanted to have fun, and I didn't think I deserved this kind of guy, either. Eric was too good to be true, and past relationships had damaged me. How Eric treated me felt strange compared to how other guys treated me. I felt like I didn't deserve it, and that was crazy. I didn't deserve Eric.

I know it sounds insane, but sometimes we do that to ourselves because we don't believe we deserve a great thing, or you don't know your self-worth. When you have unhealed trauma, it shows up in many ways, and you will self-sabotage healthy, safe relationships unknowingly until you address the trauma and heal from the past. I didn't know my self-worth because I ended up giving up on Eric to talk back to my ex, Dre.

CHAPTER 3

"I'M A MOTHER OF AN AUTISTIC SON"

After breaking my engagement, I began talking with Dre again; he was my way to forget about Eric and not address the real problem that was going on. It began to get serious with Dre. I was spending more time at his place, he was spending more time at mine, a bit too much because pretty soon, my cycle was late, and I was six weeks pregnant.

I didn't know how to feel about being pregnant. I knew for sure that I didn't want to get an abortion, and I knew that I was going to hurt and disappoint a few people, and I did. I remember telling Dre that I was pregnant, and he was upset. He didn't want me to keep it at all! I found out that he had another kid on the way with his son's mother, and she was expecting another one in a couple of months. Right then, I knew that I would have to take care of this child on my own because Dre wasn't about to be a part of my child's life.

Next, I 'm going to let my parents know. My dad wasn't mad at me as I thought he would have been. He told me to be ready to take care of the baby on my own because I can't depend on the father to help me. My mother's attitude was entirely different, and she told me not to ask her to do anything because it was my responsibility. Hearing that hurt! I was expecting a little more compassion or empathy. I felt like I was a disappointment to my mom and that I was messing up my future by getting pregnant when that wasn't the case at all.

I still had to tell my ex-fiancé that I was pregnant, and it wasn't his. Yeah, I know you 're saying, "Trae, you trifling," and I'm going to have to say, "Yes, I was very trifling." I was broken and hurt by past relationships and never healed from them. I didn't care who I was hurting because I didn't care about myself, but I had to change my mindset because I had to take care of someone other than me.

My pregnancy had changed my perspective; it was no longer about me. Now I had to take care of myself and a child. I remember when I found out that I was having a boy. I was at work when I started having horrible cramping. I called the advice nurse, and she told me to go to the hospital and check it out. I arrived in the emergency room, and I was seen quickly. Everything was alright with the baby and me, and everything turned out to be okay. Then the nurse asked if I wanted to know what I was going to have. Yes, I did want to know. She said, "I think you're having a boy." I was upset! I only wanted a girl. I believe I cried because I didn't want a boy. I wanted a girl. I had to tell myself that God gives you what you need, not what you want, so I embraced the fact that I would have a healthy baby boy. I never thought that a couple of weeks later, I would go into labor.

My son was born at 25 weeks and weighed 1 pound 11 ounces. He was deemed an extremely premature baby and remained in the hospital for three months. He weighed 4 pounds when he got home. Due to complications, Jaylen would be coming home with a heart monitor and nebulizer for breathing treatments along with several different medications. He had several various doctor appointments a week, and he also had a nurse come to our home. Being a single mom to a premature baby was my new normal, and I did it on my own. I was doing this by myself during the day and would get help from my family at night so that I could work nights.

Jaylen was a sweet baby; he just cried when he was hungry, wet, sleepy, or not feeling well. I didn't have an issue with him, and I thought he was the perfect baby. Jaylen got older and developed more, and some things were a little more delayed than others, so his doctors thought we should meet with a development specialist to see if the interventions would help his delayed development. So now, he'd have to go to a physical therapist, occupational therapist, and speech therapist to help with his progress, and this type of intervention lasted for three years.

Upon getting the intervention, I found a change in his growth; my son still didn't talk that much to others, but he spoke at home. Now it was time for him to start going to public school, and this is where we began to see Jaylen's behavior problems and other sorts of unusual behavior. The behavioral issues have been aggression towards other children, falling, crying, and screaming. The teacher saw that he would play by himself in the playground, that he would not make eye contact, and that he would repeat everything. She asked if I had noticed this behavior? At first, I didn't recognize it, then slowly, I began to see it after it was brought to my attention. I notified his doctor, and his doctor directed us to the Autism Disorder Specialist. It took about six months to have an appointment, then about three months to get seen. During this time is where I developed patience with myself, my son, and others. He was finally able to get tested, and they found out that he did have autism and that he also had ADHD. Autism is a pervasive developmental disorder that involves abnormal development and function of the brain. People with autism show decreased social communication skills and restricted or repetitive patterns of behavior or interests. Attention Deficit Hyperactivity Disorder (ADHD) is a neurodevelopmental disorder. It is usually diagnosed for the first time in childhood and often lasts into adulthood. Children with ADHD may have difficulty paying attention, managing impulsive actions, or being overactive.

After finding out my son had ASD and ADHD, I felt so ashamed and embarrassed. I didn't want anyone to know that my son had a difference. Knowing that he had autism was a hard pill to swallow, but it wasn't about me, it was about my son. I needed to be sure that he could reach his full ability, and I wanted to be sure that my son would receive the necessary resources and programs that would help him in the longer term.

To be honest with you all, I wanted to quit too many times, but God would not let me give up. Having a child with autism is a different kind of parenting. You always need to explain yourself, do the same thing repeatedly, everything must be structured, there are no last-minute changes, and if you do, you may have a huge problem. Only parents that have kids with autism or other differences will understand what I'm saying. Being an ASD parent is not easy; I make it look easy. I made so many sacrifices to make sure my son would not have to suffer or feel ashamed of his differences, and today, he has become an amazing young man with a bright future ahead of him.

CHAPTER 4

I LEFT HIM, HE NEVER LEFT ME

I've been in church all my life. Growing up as a preacher's kid, you get your fair share of the church. Every day of the week was something. Monday was the only day I didn't have church. Tuesday through Sunday, I had Bible study, prayer meeting, choir rehearsal, usher board meeting, a musical or Revival, and back to Church on Sunday morning and maybe even Sunday night service; it was never-ending. The church was how I grew up, and all I knew was the church, so it didn't bother me because this was my norm. It was the "not going" to Church I didn't understand and how could you "stay home" or do "something else" on a Sunday other than going to Church I couldn't process. However, as I got older and I got out on my own and wanted to explore what life was about, something had to give, and my life was not about to be the one that I give up. I was going to give up church because I had been in church all my life.

By the age of 20, I was tired of the church! I wanted to live my life now. The church was all I knew; my parents allowed me to experience certain things in life, which was great, because it allowed me to see things from different perspectives, but I wanted to see and do what my friends were doing. By now, I could choose if I wanted to go to church or not go to church, so I wasn't going as often. I wasn't taking the Ministry seriously anymore. I gave up teaching youth and young adult Bible study, and I didn't want to direct or sing in the choir anymore.

My boyfriend at the time became my distraction and focus. I was starting to party and work, and if it wasn't any of these, I did not care about it. I even started smoking weed again, which was now a daily routine; life was about to go downhill from here. I wasn't hanging around the people that would hold me accountable for my actions like my church family, so I began to spiral out of control, and this behavior lasted for a while. It's not like I didn't know right from wrong. I was just running from myself because I didn't want to face my reality, and my reality was the church. I would eventually get pregnant, and I would find my way back to church.

Getting back in the church didn't feel the same, the people in my church home had left or were barely coming, and I had outgrown the teaching. I did not want to stop going to church, so I had to make a decision and make it quick. So, after going to the church, I had called my home, and my family and I left and went somewhere else.

Attending another church for the first time in my life, I did not know anyone, and no one knew me. This church was different from the traditional church I was used to, so it took me a while to adjust. The pastor and his wife were young, and their kids were around my son's age, so this was perfect. The teaching I was receiving was Bible-based, and the pastor kept it real, he did not sugarcoat anything, and no subject was off-limits. I just knew this was wrong, or could I have been taught wrong growing up? Growing up in church, we didn't talk about sex and relationships, managing your money, everyday life struggles, and other topics that made you uncomfortable or prepared you for life. For the kingdom, it just wasn't happening, but at this new church, no topic was off-limits.

I found myself growing in Christ, going home every Sunday satisfied, knowing that I was going to get through the week and having the resources and tools to get me through. I could be myself, with no judgment, never feeling ashamed about my past mistakes, nor were they thrown back into my face. I was being held accountable for my actions in the body of Christ, and it felt good to have a relationship with God again, finally.

When I stopped going to church, my life started to get out of control, and I started doing the things I'd stopped doing. In my eyes, God wasn't working fast enough, and I needed to help speed things up when it came to my life. Well, I will tell you this; God does not need your help; he is doing just fine without your help. When you surrender your life to God, your life is not your life anymore. Your time is not your time; it is God's time now. What you used to do; you can't do anymore. Yep! Sleeping around, smoking weed, or hanging around the wrong crowd, you can't do it anymore and have a relationship with God and think that it's okay to live this way. It's not, and you will find yourself repeating the same cycle that you got yourself out of, so you will have to choose. Is it hard? Yes, it is; it's one of the hardest things that I struggle with daily.

There are things that you can do to help with your struggle that helped me with mine. I started to surround myself with people who wanted to live the same lifestyle as I did or who were already living God's way. I have people in my life who will hold me accountable for my actions and the choices that I make. I don't rush my decisions. I ask God about his plans for me, and lastly, I left the old ways of life and now try my best to live on the path of love. This lifestyle is not for everyone, but I can tell you this; it's for me, and I wouldn't change it for the world. At the end of the day, it's your decision if you decide, but if I can encourage you, I will say do it and trust God.

CHAPTER 5

EMOTIONAL DRIVEN RELATIONSHIPS

I went through so many things when it comes to relationships, some of the things I caused, some of the things I allowed, and some were just stupid, and I had no reason getting into in the first place. I found myself in and out of the same relationship pattern with different guys, doing what I told myself I would never do again. And I would find myself doing the thing I said I would not do, so much so I didn't realize I was in the same type of relationship for many years with different dudes. Some would last a year or more, and the ones that lasted a year or more were the hardest to get out of.

I was in a relationship with this guy named Drew for 5 years, and I didn't realize I was in an emotionally abusive relationship. He would go out of his way to show me attention, love, and affection. He bought me gifts and showed romantic gestures, but this was just to hook me. He showed me his protective side and would get a little jealous if another guy would look at me when we were out together, but in a joking way, so I thought. The protectiveness and subtle jealousies turned into possessiveness. He would get paranoid and required that I always be accessible. Any time that he text or called me, he expected me to answer right away. He always questioned my whereabouts, who I was with, and what I did. Still, I ignored the red flags that were right in my face.

I first met Drew when I moved to West Oakland. I would never give Drew the time of day. I ignored him for five years until this one day, he appeared and approached me differently, and that's when I gave him a chance. He was nice-looking, tall, slim, had a nice body and a smile you would fall for. He was sweet, very protective, supportive, always making me laugh, he loved my son, and he loved me. I thought that this was enough because I didn't require more from him, and I didn't think I deserved better because of all the dirt I had already done to guys, so I just settled. I ended up settling for someone who lied, cheated and emotionally abused me.

We had been together for a year and a half before I found out about his true lifestyle, and what he had been telling me and what I was seeing was all a lie. He had lost his job in construction, so he started back selling drugs, selling gift cards and doing check-cashing schemes. I even found out he did Fed time, committing white-collar crimes. I only found out because he caught a case and went to jail, and he called collect. But that wasn't the only thing I found out. I also found out that he was married but separated from his wife, and he had more children than what he told me. Finding out all this stuff hurt like hell; it was like I did not know the person I was dating, but would I leave him? Naw! I continued this relationship for a few more years because I could not get out, and every time I tried, he would say something that would get me to stay.

He knew everywhere I went, not because I told him, but because he had people following me and keeping tabs on me. If anyone dared to look my way or get at me (flirt), and he found out about it, he would have something done to them. Anybody that would come to my house, Drew would get their license plate number and find out who they were, where they lived and what they did for a living. Drew had so many connections, it was crazy.

I began to realize that I was in a hostage relationship, and I needed a plan to get out and get away before someone got hurt or killed. I had to find a way to get out, and I did. I started looking for another place to live or programs that would help me move. I found out about the first-time homebuyer's program through the City of Oakland. I went to an orientation to find out what I needed to do, and I got started. I found out that the process would take or could take up to a year, but I tried it anyway. I was able to bypass a few steps because I had cleaned up my credit, and I didn't have any debt, so this sped up the process for me to move. I was able to get approved for a $250,000 loan, now all I had to do was look for a house. I would hide all my information, so Drew wouldn't know what I was planning. I still played the role of girlfriend and pretended that I still loved him, pretended like everything was cool because I did not want him to suspect anything.

I started looking for a house, and I found one in West Oakland. It wasn't that far, but Drew didn't know anything. Now it was time for me to move out of my apartment, and it was good timing as Drew had gone out of town for the weekend. I closed on my house, and I could move in. I packed up my house, cleaned it up and was gone. I broke away from a relationship that was killing me mentally and had I stayed any longer; I would have been killing myself. You may be saying, "Trae, this doesn't make sense, you're smarter than that." Well, I wasn't. I stayed because I thought this dude was going to change, or I could help change him. Ladies and gentlemen, if they don't want to change for themselves, you can't make them change, and as much as you love them, you need to love yourself a little bit more to get out. Trust the red flags that you see when you first start dating and confront them. Don't push them under the rug because it's not going to go anywhere. It will begin to form something that you won't be able to handle or control.

CHAPTER 6

THE THINGS I ALLOWED

A lot of us get into relationships that start with casual text messages that lead to long conversations, and those intense conversations can quickly take us away from the simple reality about how we feel and what we need. You're making time for that person, you're always engaging with each other, nothing that person does bothers you and the connection feels natural. The chemistry is there, so you say, "That is it!" Then you feel like the other individual is either pulling away or becoming more controlling. Your "good morning, have an amazing day" texts are becoming less and less frequent or end, and you feel as if you guys are beginning to fade from each other. For me, this happened in the first part of my relationship with Julian, who I met through a mutual friend. He was different from other dudes; we had so many similarities, and what made me think we were a good match was that we could converse about anything. No subject was off-limits, and we spent a lot of time together in the beginning, getting to know one another.

It started well; we were together all the time, almost every day. We talked and texted as if we were in high school. He told me that he was in love with me in the first month of dating, and he told me how pretty I was and how compatible we were. He said all the right things to get me. But I soon learned that this was his way to cover up his self-doubt and his insecurities and flaws.

Julian portrayed himself as always having his life together, so he could never be wrong and expected those around him to agree with him and his point of view. He became quickly angered and would blow things out of proportion to get out of doing something or be kept accountable for his actions. I ignored these things in the beginning.

He took advantage of my caring nature and my willingness to do things for others. Julian knew how empathetic I was, and he took my kindness for weakness. I didn't have an issue sharing personal thoughts with him either and he made it feel like we were connecting. But, in fact, he took my personal information and used it against me when we had arguments. Another red flag that I chose to disregard. Eventually, it was something that I couldn't ignore.

I don't know what happened to Julian to cheat on me in our relationship; it just happened. I remember when I found out, I had just left Sacramento State to head back to Oakland. Usually, Julian would call me, but for some reason, that day, he didn't. I called him, and the conversation was hella dry, and I was like, "Is everything alright with you?" He instantly got defensive, and he was like, "I don't have time for all these questions, and I'm really getting tired of you!" I didn't want to press the issue, so I left it alone. I was thinking, "What did I do? Did I say something wrong?" The truth was I had done nothing wrong. He was trying to create something, so we could break up and stop talking to one another.

Late that evening, Julian came to my house because he needed to talk, and that's when he told me that he had gotten his "baby mama" pregnant by mistake, and she was due in a couple of months. He didn't want me to find out on social media, but he felt the need to tell me. I was crushed because it had happened to me again. It was evident that I had to do some soul-searching and get down to the root of the problem on why this same kind of situation had happened to me again. Why hadn't I paid attention to the red flags? Fool me once, shame on you to fool me twice, shame on me, because this time it was definitely shame on me.

What I've allowed myself to go through is hurtful and embarrassing. Still, through that hurt and embarrassment, I found the courage to tell what I allowed myself to go through or the chaos I created. Early in a relationship, you have a choice to continue whether things are good or not. You have the option of being treated with respect and the alternative to being mistreated, and I chose to be mistreated, cheated on, lied to, disrespected, humiliated, and much more, just because I didn't want to be lonely. I didn't believe I could do better or expect better, so I stayed in the complicated relationships, knowing that I was being cheated on, lied to, emotionally abused, among other things. These were huge red flags that I ignored and swept under the rug, all because I was afraid to be lonely, and there was more to come!

At some point, you must find the strength to leave an unhealthy relationship. You deserve to be happy, and you deserve to be in a healthy relationship with someone who truly cares about you. Allow yourself time to heal before you enter another relationship because it is essential to give yourself time to heal mentally and recover from being in a toxic relationship. Surround yourself with positive people that won't allow you to victimize yourself but instead, view yourself as a strong individual, who can get through this. Do not be afraid of sharing your story or feel shame for what you experienced because telling your story could save someone's life. Lastly, seek professional help if necessary, as this will help you get to the root of the problem, and you can begin healing from within and start loving yourself. Don't allow that person to keep a piece of your heart forever.

CHAPTER 7

SURVIVING TOXIC RELATIONSHIPS

By now, you can see that I have been in some very unhealthy relationships, some lasting for years, and some lasting for just a few months. An unhealthy relationship can be physical, emotional, or verbal abuse. It can look like control, someone who tells you what to do, what to wear, and who to hang out. It can also look like humiliation, someone who calls you out, puts you down or makes you feel bad in front of other people. It can also be unpredictable behavior like getting angry quickly to the point where you don't know what will set them off, so it feels like you're walking on eggshells around them. There's a range of unhealthy characteristics, but I will stick with these for now.

I've never been in a physically abusive relationship, and I thank God I've never been in one; however, I have been in other types of abusive relationships. Now, the questions are, how did I get myself into this, and why did I stay? What took me so long to get out? And how did I get out?

When I first started each relationship, I never took the time to get to know the person I was dating; it was a rushed relationship. I had sex way too early in the relationship and didn't have the opportunity to get to know them before deciding to have sex with them. I didn't give the relationship time to build emotional intimacy, which caused problems in the relationships. If you have sex with someone soon after you encounter them, you might give a message that sex is just what you want. When you don't have the time to get to know somebody first, they believe you don't even care to know them, and this is how I felt some of the time and other times, I did dudes like dudes do some females and just sent him on their way and didn't look back.

One thing I did wrong in my relationship is, we moved in together too soon. The crazy part is this wasn't part of my upbringing, my parents were married, so I don't know why I thought that this was okay. I was shacking up with my dude, which wasn't cool. I was acting as if I was married, cooking and cleaning, taking care of the kids, and all the sex I wanted. We became codependent too quickly and didn't know how to create appropriate boundaries, which caused insecurities in the relationship for both of us. Even though we came home to each other every night, there was still a lack of trust, which caused a rift in our relationship.

These rifts in our relationship didn't make me leave, and I overlooked all the red flags just to say I was in a relationship. I didn't want to be lonely, and I didn't know how to be by myself. I had to make people think I was okay and happy because if you're in a relationship, it can sometimes let people know that you're alright, so I thought. After all, you are dating. But deep down inside, everything is not okay; I was hella broken in every way too. I was trying to avoid feeling that uncomfortable brokenness, so I stayed with the "wrong" person to help me avoid looking at myself and healing correctly. Another reason why I stayed is I wanted to show my loyalty, and I believed I could change the person I was dating, and I was not giving up on my investment. Since then, I have learned that sometimes, you must lose to win to live to see another day and doing that may shape you into character and help define your purpose.

There was no easy way to get out of these relationships. I gave myself a lot of excuses to stay, but the bottom line is that when I allowed someone to view me as less valuable than I am, my self-esteem was fatally wounded. When your self-worth is weak, it's easy for your ex to get over the wall of your good defenses and steal what's left of your confidence. Finding the strength to remove yourself from these unhealthy situations and surrounding yourself with supportive people are the best actions you can take and love yourself enough to leave.

CHAPTER 8

LIVING MY BEST LIFE

As individuals, some of our deepest-rooted wants and needs are to have a fulfilling and enjoyable life. For me, to live the best experience implies being free to do what you want, and circumstances don't deter you from doing that. Many of us dream of a better future, such as getting your own home someday, a profession you enjoy, a decent education, or a variety of things. These were just some of the things that were going to get me to live my best life. There were some obstacles that I went through to achieve the goals I set for myself. I had to give up a few things, place my trust in God, have faith, and believe that He would bring me through, and sometimes, trusting God is not always easy.

Self-growth reaching new heights and seeking purpose were all ideas of what I needed to care about when I had my son. I couldn't imagine myself raising my son in an apartment, only having a high school education, and just working some old job. I aspired for more.

One of the first things I did was go back into college and take it seriously this time. I decided to take two to three classes at a time, met with instructors and counselors to make sure that I was passing my courses and to be sure that I was taking the necessary courses to graduate. I was finally in the right direction and fulfilling my personal goals, and by 2008, I had completed my A.A. in Liberal Arts and an A.S. in Sociology. I was on my way to Sacramento State College to major in Criminal Justice.

The next goal I set for myself was to buy my own house by 30, and it wasn't easy; it seemed to take forever, even though it wasn't. I was living in public housing, and the environment was becoming dangerous, and I couldn't bear it anymore, not to mention the need to get away from my boyfriend. A couple of years before I decided to move, the townhome adjacent to mine was shot up, and two people were killed. After that incident, I was ready to go but couldn't because of my finances at the time, so I had to wait.

One day, I received a notice regarding a first-time homebuyer program. The Housing Authority I was living in was organizing an informational meeting and encouraged people to participate, so I went and got some beneficial information and took advantage of the opportunity. There were a lot of people telling me not to take advantage of this program because I wouldn't be the one that owned the property, the city would own the home, but that wasn't necessarily true. The catch was, I needed to stay in the house for 15 years, and after the 15 years, the loan would be forgiven. It was during the 2008 recession when I began this process. Many people were losing their jobs and home, but I was about to purchase a home, and I had two jobs; that was nothing but God. I was approved for a $250,000 loan, but I was only able to buy in Oakland. It took eight months and two realtors before I purchased my first home for my 30th birthday, and my son and I were finally able to live part of the American dream.

To achieve similar goals like mine, you have to be willing to make sacrifices, and those sacrifices could be your personal life, your stability, and maybe your faith. It may take unexpected turns to follow your dreams, but these are the exciting and memorable challenges of living your best life. Your dreams and your actions define you. Don't let others define you with what they tell you to do and not to do. You will inspire others to follow their dreams, even if they know nothing about you.

CHAPTER 9

THE DAY THAT NEVER CAME

Imagine, the person you're going out with proposed to you, you announce it to family and friends and set a date. You pick a venue to have your wedding and select your wedding party. You pick out your wedding dress, take engagement photos and stamps are on all your invitations to be sent out. Three months before the wedding, you get a text message from your fiancé, letting you know that they can't go on with the wedding.

This occurred in 2011 when I started talking back to this dude named Devin. Devin was tall, attractive, friendly, and knew when to take control. He was reserved and only hung out with few people but was well-known. A lot of people thought we made a cute couple because our personalities went well with each other, and we looked so happy together. We met in high school and dated for a while after I graduated.

We were always together; if I wasn't at his place, he was at mine, or we would be together, hanging out with our mutual friends. At one stage in the relationship, I had issues at home, and he helped me suppress the things I was going through at home. So instead of talking about what was going on, I would just deny it and say, "everything's fine, let's all go out." He thought that he could get away with things by seeing this passive side of me, and since I don't address them or hold him accountable for his actions towards me, he felt he could get away with things, and that's when the relationship started to go downhill.

Devin would eventually cheat on me, and I found out because something didn't feel right. He would ask that I drop him off early and pick him up later than usual. He then became too busy to hang out, and our time together was limited. Devin and my cousin worked with each other, so I threatened my cousin and his friend to tell me, and they told me everything. I hopped in my car and drove to the spot where they told me the female lived, and I waited for him to arrive. He finally arrived, and as I was about to hop out, the chick that he was with got out of the car too, and she looked like she was 7 or 8 months pregnant. My heart was so broken. I was devastated because I'd had an abortion 7 or 8 months back. We thought that we were both too young to have a baby, so we chose another option. After finding that he was having a baby, I left him alone.

Years later, we discovered each other on social media and started to have casual conversations, and those interactions led to more in-depth discussions that prompted us to date again. We spoke about our history, and he apologized for what he had done, and we began dating. Devin proposed in December 2011; it wasn't your traditional way of getting down on one knee. We were at his place, and we were talking about marriage, and he came out and asked if I'd marry him. I think I asked him again if he was serious because he would often play too much, but this time he was serious, and I said yes.

I was so excited that I was actually going to get married, so we began preparing for the wedding and set a date for January 12, 2013. At first, I didn't want a wedding; I just wanted to go to the courthouse and have a beautiful reception, but Devin wanted the wedding at the golf course, so that's what we did. We chose a location, placed a down payment for the wedding venue, selected the wedding party, and the color scheme for the wedding.

As the wedding day grew closer, I started having crazy dreams of my wedding day, and I would wake up gasping for air, after dreaming he would end up leaving me at the altar. Dreams have ways of warning you even before the events occur, so when you receive those warnings, I think you should pay attention to them. I didn't. I continued with planning the wedding, even though something wasn't right deep inside. The store where I was purchasing my wedding dress went abruptly out of business, and I had one day to get my wedding dress or risk losing it three months before I got married. Some of my bridesmaids hadn't gotten their dresses yet, and they came up with excuses as to why they hadn't purchased them. I recall one day when I was sitting alone on my back porch, and I heard a voice say, "You're not getting married. I turned around because it sounded like somebody was standing behind me, but no one was there. Three weeks after I heard that voice, I got a text message from Devin, saying he couldn't get married.

At first, I was hella mad, and I couldn't believe that had happened to me, I was hurt. It took everything to refrain from going off on Devin. This felt like I was in a terrible nightmare, but I couldn't wake up from it. I had so many thoughts and impulses that I couldn't handle mentally, and to make matters worse, I had to inform my family and friends that the wedding was off. Every call was worse than the last one, and my heart broke in more pieces with every call. I still needed to contact the venue to let them know that I wasn't going to need it. Because the money was not refundable, I either had to lose the money or use it on something else, so I opted to throw my mother and aunt a birthday party on the day I was scheduled to be married.

I thought I'd get a sense of closure by having this party so I could move forward with the rest of my life, but it wasn't. I honestly didn't know the real reason why the engagement ended. I was still holding on to the emotional attachment, which resulted in no closure. Because of this, I didn't give myself the chance to develop a new and healthy relationship with anyone after this, which wasn't fair to myself or the next person I dated.

This has affected me in so many ways. I felt unloved, insignificant, and my self-esteem was weak. I just thought there was something wrong with me, so I blamed myself. My role in all this was the enabler; I allowed this behavior and treatment he showed to me, and I gave in to whatever it was to keep him around.

I've never fully healed from this experience and brought this trauma into the next relationships that I was in. I realized that in future relationships, I need to establish trust and respect, and create boundaries to communicate my needs and wants. I realize now that love is not enough. There are so many other aspects that are required for a good relationship. Hence, I've learned to sprint quickly when red flags show up.

CHAPTER 10

BROKEN

You can only ignore the reality about yourself for so long until others begin to see the true you. Your chaos and imperfections, you are untrusting, struggling with fear, anxiety, or worry. You may have a rough time expressing love without reacting with frustration, or you may feel lost in your life. What I just described was some brokenness. I've had so many challenges, but I've kept going despite everything I've gone through. I didn't realize I was broken until it was too late, and let me say, being broken isn't terrible; it's how you transform your brokenness is what matters most.

Because of the past hurt and never really taking the time to heal correctly, I had a hard time trusting the opposite sex. Some of the guys I let know, and some I didn't. The hurt I've experienced, I had a choice to either process the pain, allow myself to heal, and remain open to trust, but I did the opposite. I ran from relationship to relationship because I didn't want to give myself time to process the pain that was caused in most of them.

By doing this, I didn't give myself a chance to heal correctly, so I could trust, be honest, and have compassion, which could be the things you need to have in a healthy relationship. In some of these relationships, I was genuinely in love, and in others, it was all lust.

1 John 4:18 says, "He who fears has not been made perfect in love." The guys I truly loved I didn't struggle with fear, anxiety, nor did I worry. But the ones I lusted over, I battled with fear, anxiety, and worry, which caused brokenness and created a void. I struggled to love because I was lacking and unable to love, which would make love challenging to process. Some that loved me, I didn't display any emotion or affection because I couldn't take the love they were giving. I've been heartbroken so many times that I've started to distance myself emotionally in a relationship to protect myself from being hurt. This behavior would surface in most, if not all, of my relationships, which would leave me afraid and unwilling to love.

This brokenness kept me stuck in the same dysfunctional pattern of relationships for years, so long it felt normal with each connection. Like attracting emotionally unavailable people or in relationships, being unable to communicate about things that bother me, being a "Caregiver" or mistaking love for physical attraction, neediness, and the need to rescue or be rescued, I hoped for different results. Still, they would always turn out the same way. I kept these patterns going because I knew that anything else would be unfamiliar and uncomfortable. I chose the familiar and comfortable path because I didn't want to repair my heart at the time, so I repeated the same dysfunctional pattern to play it safe.

To heal from my brokenness, I had to be willing to reflect on each relationship to see what caused my behavior to change and figure out where it all began. I also had to realize that I was responsible for my actions and the practice I had learned and then learn healthier ways.

The first thing I had to do was forgive myself for all the times I'd entered a relationship that wasn't healthy, that left me feeling hurt, unworthy, or unnoticed, or that made me damage others. I then had to do the next painful thing, asking myself questions to get a full understanding of how the pattern came about. I had to figure out exactly what all these relationships have in common? What were some of the warning signs I'd ignored earlier in the relationship? What behavior patterns have all these relationships brought out of me, over and over and over again? Lastly, what was it about those relationships that triggered such behaviors in me? Understanding where the pattern originated from and how it formed was the secret to discovering ways to break bad relationship patterns.

Then it was time to look at some of the red flags that I'd missed in the past, so I could easily recognize them if they showed up again. I wanted to feel wanted. I wanted my man to love me and give me protection. And that always led me to a relationship with possessive and manipulating men, and before I knew it, I was back into an old pattern. You need to look hard for these types of signs because they can be disguised as attractive things that lure you in like bait. You have to be able to identify the warning signs, so you won't get trapped so easily.

I was my worst enemy. I was the one who enabled these dudes to abuse me in any shape or form, and no woman or man should ever allow that to happen to them. I was broken, and being broken is nothing to be embarrassed about, not accepting your brokenness is what you ought to be scared of. Seek guidance so that you can get to the root of the problem; I know I did when I realized that I was repeating the same patterns. Now, ask yourself, how did I end up here? Why am

I attracting the same kind of people? Is it worth it, or am I worth more? The lesson I learned, and you can, too, is that you have to be broken sometimes so that God could put me back together again.

CHAPTER 11

LOOKING FOR LOVE IN THE WRONG PEOPLE

Love is a four-letter word that we often say to a person, about a place or an object. It can be defined as an overwhelming feeling or a deep appreciation. Love can be so many beautiful things if you experience it correctly. However, it can also be manipulated into a disguise and made to seem like love if someone doesn't realize the true meaning or has never been shown what love truly is. I always thought I saw it in a guy named Kailen, who I dated for three and a half years, but if you don't love or value yourself, you can't trust anyone to appreciate or love you the way you should be loved.

I met Kailen in high school, and we also worked at the same job for a couple of years, and during that time, we would say hello and speak from time to time, but nothing too significant until we became friends on social media. I remember making a post about having to go to a Mexican restaurant, but I didn't want to go by myself, so instead of commenting on the post, he decided to message me. We messaged back and forth and made arrangements to see each other that weekend.

When the weekend came, I wasn't sure whether it was a date, or maybe two old friends who were hanging out. I was hesitant to go out with him due to the past dates I'd been on. We met at the restaurant, and we caught up on each other's lives and just hung out. It was fun. We talked for about five hours in the restaurant and spent another hour in the parking lot talking. I would see Kailen again in a few days and begin a friendship, which would turn into a relationship. Dating him was fun and crazy at the same time in the beginning. We got along so well, and I didn't see any red flags that said leave now and don't look back.

There was a passion for Kailen, both emotional and physical. We had several things in common, our world views were close, and our sense of humor was a match. Kailen didn't have any children, so he didn't bring any "baby mama "drama; he had never been married and had been out of a serious relationship for some time. He held two jobs and had been working both for more than ten years and had never been arrested or incarcerated. It was as though I had found a diamond, a precious stone, and these were some of the things I had prayed for, so I was satisfied.

Our first year of dating was the honeymoon phase, so the fresh and exciting, constant learning of new things about each other, and the first experiences had suddenly come to their point, and the real Kailen had begun to show. He showed me that he wanted to keep the relationship going, or so I thought.

There was a time when we broke up for a couple of months; this was the first visible sign that I was supposed to leave and never look back. I fell asleep waiting for him to come to my house once, and instead of knocking on my door, he called my cell. I called him to let him know what happened, but he didn't answer his phone because he had his music up and probably couldn't hear his phone ring, so I waited a couple of minutes to call again, and he answered the phone mad. He said I should have told him I was going to sleep, and he wouldn't have driven to my house. He would have gone home after hanging with his friends. It was like two in the morning, and Kailen didn't knock on the door to indicate that he was at the door, and any smart person who wants to get in the house would have knocked hella hard on the door!

After Kailen told me this, and I explained to him, you would have thought that we were cool. WRONG! Instead, he wouldn't text back when I texted, and he didn't answer the phone when I called. I had to come out of character for him to reply, which nobody should do to get a response from anyone. It still didn't make much sense to me. How could a person trip off something so stupid and immature? I mean, we were adults, or at least I was.

I was trying to accept that it was over and to find myself again. I continued to hang out with friends and family, going to concerts, football games, and comedy shows. I even ran into him at a concert, looked him straight in the eye, looked him up and down, said nothing, and walked away. I also got back in the gym and dropped some weight. I looked good.

Kailen still had some belongings at my house, and before I threw them away, I messaged him on social media, asking if he wanted them, and he responded. After three months of not speaking, he finally talked to me. I wondered when or where we would meet, so I gave him his things, and instead of him getting his stuff, we talked about the break-up. I did most of the talking, and he just sat and listened. At the time, I just really missed him and wanted him back, so I didn't hold him accountable for his actions, and we got back together. Things weren't the same for me after getting back together, and the relationship never got back as it was. Don't get me wrong, we were still going out on dates and went out of town a couple of times, but for me, I noticed that his behavior had started to change. It was like I didn't know him at all. He began to hang out with his friends more, smoke weed, and drink, all the things he claimed he didn't do any more when we first got together, and it was heartbreaking to see this behavior from him that made me question: was this the real Kailen?

By now, we were in our third year of dating and approaching our fourth year, and I started to notice that the relationship was changing, but not in the direction I wanted to go in. I noticed that the relationship was beginning to be about Kailen. For example, where he wanted to go, when he wanted to see me, what Kailen wanted to do and not do, and how he felt. He would blame me for minor things that I had nothing to do with or had any control of, and he would play the victim and make me feel like I was responsible for it. Kailen would sometimes give me the silent treatment, his way of keeping me in awe of what was going on and a sure way of telling me what I did wrong and how bad it was. This was Kailen's way to keep me out of his business, but also his way of fixing the problem. Kailen would expect me to read his mind and automatically respond with understanding and compassion, which made it nearly impossible to deal with the appropriateness of what he desired, but the pressure was often felt. These were all types of controlling behavior that I saw in my relationships with Kailen. He was seeking control of me and used all these strategies, such as blame, isolation, guilt or alienation, and intimidation.

This action from Kailen was part of the explanation of why we split up, along with the lack of communication that was the last straw. I started asking him where the relationship was, and he couldn't even tell me that.

One night, when he had been out with his friends partying and smoking weed at a bonfire, he came to my house smelling like hella, smoke and alcohol, and he was so drunk and high that he passed out before he could even take a shower. He was very dismissive of this, making things easier for me to leave and not to think about losing him, and I just did that a few weeks after this happened. It was one night that I felt the need to call him out on his behavior. It was certainly out of the ordinary coming from me; I had suppressed three years' worth of thoughts and feelings, and it was time I let it out. I knew he didn't appreciate it because all he could say was, "I'll call you later." A couple of weeks after, he lied about being with his friends, so I hung up in his face and never contacted him again. By now, I had felt like I'd wasted hella time and managed to slip back to the same toxic relationship cycle that I told myself that I'd never find myself in. This time, instead of feeling sorry for myself, I wanted to get to the root of this problem. I didn't want to give Kailen any more power or be inclined to feel vindictive against the guy who had taken up my time and energy. I couldn't go around berating myself for not noticing the signs significantly earlier. I couldn't allow this to limit my perspective, which would stagnate my personal growth further.

I had to change my mindset from a negative to a positive mindset. I also had to realize that this relationship was a learning opportunity and thank Kailen for this opportunity to identify what I will and will not accept in future relationships.

The next thing I didn't want to ignore any longer was how I kept getting myself back into toxic relationships? What it led me back to was me not fully healing from past relationships and unresolved hurt that I had suppressed for many years, which caused an unhealthy relationship pattern that turned into unhealthy beliefs. I needed to be free from unhealthy beliefs and identify the lie that was holding me hostage. I learned that I was emotionally unhealthy, and I looked to Kailen for my happiness and love. How could I expect that from someone who wasn't raised to realize what love was? He'd failed in previous relationships and would probably make the same mistake again until he identified the fears that were keeping him from moving towards healthy love.

Ultimately, we can't hold anyone accountable for our happiness. We've got to take full responsibility for that. If you don't, you may be attaching your hopes, dreams, weaknesses, and uncertainties to this person who is not responsible for this, and you can be continually disappointed by love.

CHAPTER 12

THE MASK I WORE

Some of us may have a routine that we do every morning; you roll out of bed, use the restroom, brush your teeth, wash your face, eat breakfast, or have a cup of coffee or tea. You grab your things, and before you leave, you take a look in the mirror and unknowingly put on your mask that will cover up the pain, shame, or fear. What if I told you that you're not alone? I did the same thing day after day. My mask helped me become someone else because I was too much for some, so I would conform to make others comfortable while I was uncomfortable. I even wore the "runaway" mask because I didn't want to be the center of attention, address any conflicts, or feel rejected in any way, shape, or form. These masks paralyzed me from being my true self and leaving people wondering where or who the real Trae is.

Some of the first masks I placed on were being someone different because I was "too much" for some people. For example, if anyone asked for my opinion, I would never sugarcoat what was on my mind; I kept it real. Another instance is that certain people would get upset because how I addressed people when they spoke to me in a tone that I didn't agree with. Or even some felt that I was standoffish because I'm selective of who I chose to be friends with, so I put on the mask to not appear this way. What I had to realize was when others do these things to others, they're the person that likely disowned a certain part within themselves and is now projecting that unwanted attribute/characteristic onto you.

The next masks were easy to put on, but it was hella hard to remove. The mask of conformity was the longest one I wore. I thought that once I turned 18, my parents or others wouldn't try to tell me what to do. However, I was wrong; I thought of myself as an independent individual who chose to live the way I wanted to, without having to worry about things like that. Some might have, but for me, that's just not the case. I spent most of my adult life trying to please my mother, guys I dated, and even some friends but forgot who mattered the most, me. I would do what they decided to do or go wherever they chose to go or do what they felt was better for me. It wasn't that I didn't know how to speak for myself; I just wanted to please those I loved, even if I wasn't happy.

I had to realize that I could not please everyone, and I couldn't allow others to control parts of my life, especially if theirs weren't intact. Some people try to conform you to the image they want you to be to make themselves feel better, and they will continue if you allow them. It can be hurtful; some people who say they love you can try to change parts of you because of the insecurities they have yet to fix within themselves.

These masks didn't do anything for me but stopped me from being who I really was; never give someone that much power over your life. You have to place boundaries, so people will know your limits and true feelings. Be direct, so they know where you stand on a certain matter, so there's no confusion. When people continually decide to change you or try to adjust your behavior to avoid being hurt themselves, it's not you; it is them that needs to change. You can always say no to unwanted foolishness. Be yourself and own your flaws, your weaknesses, and the things that make you shine. You don't need anyone's approval, but remember that if someone is working hard to manipulate, it's because they probably need yours.

CHAPTER 13

LEARNING DISABILITY TO GETTING MY MASTER'S

Succeeding in school has always been a challenge for me, so I never thought that I would end up with a Master's degree. Some may breeze through school with no problems, but for others, not so much. I'm the other. I have dyslexia; if you're not familiar with that, it's a learning disorder with difficulty reading due to problems identifying speech sound and decoding. Statistics have said that a staggering 15% of Americans have dyslexia, that's about 14.5 to 43.5 million children and adults, according to the Society of Neuroscience *(Hudson, R. F., High, L., & Otaiba, S. A. (n.d.).*

I didn't know that I was dyslexic until my first year at college. I recall talking to my godmother to express my apprehension regarding attending college and how I didn't want to go because of the struggles I'd encountered in middle and high school. I just saw myself failing. My godmother noticed something special about me and said that I could do great if I just received support. She introduced me to a program at the College of Alameda that could help me out. They pointed me in the right direction to get the help I needed, and this is where I found out that I was dyslexic.

At first, I was embarrassed and ashamed, and then I became angry that I'd had a learning disability all these years. I just floated through the education system and did not receive adequate and necessary services that could have been of benefit to my life. I can recall being pulled out by resource teachers, receiving help with reading, and attending Saturday school. Still, once I got to middle and high school, it stopped. So throughout those years of school, I struggled.

Nevertheless, I didn't give up; I took advantage of opportunities available at my high school. I enrolled in the morning and afterschool class to keep me ahead of the school year. I attended summer school or went to a community college to stay ahead and not fall behind. It worked, and by the second half of my senior year of high school, I only had four classes. I was out of school after lunch, and these were the things I did on my own, not even knowing the real reason I honestly struggled.

Once I got tested at the College of Alameda, I was finally

able to receive services for my learning differences. I was able to have a note-taker, got extra time on my test, and other services that were available to set me up to succeed in college. During my first year in college, I did not take it seriously. I was disorganized; I hung out with friends and skipped class, never studied, and was distracted easily. I changed my degree major a few times, especially when things were not going well or had become too hard for me, and on top of all of that, I was barely passing my classes, so I dropped out of school.

It wasn't until I had my son that I went back to college. My attitude had shifted, so I was taking it more seriously. I finally decided that I would major in criminal justice, so I enrolled in full-time classes at Merritt College and worked part-time at night. I was finally feeling like I was accomplishing things and finally had my dyslexia under control; I was doing very well in school. I had become very organized, and I wasn't hanging out with friends. My study habits had improved, I wasn't easily distracted, and I was passing all my courses. I also checked in with my instructors and often met with my counselors to make sure that I was on track to either graduate or transfer to a university or state college. After all the hard work, I earned an A.A. in Liberal Arts and A.S. in Sociology. I was able to transfer to

Sacramento State, where I earned my bachelor's degree in Criminal Justice.

By now, I was utterly exhausted from going to school. However, I was wrong, and I didn't feel accomplished academically. I thought that I still needed to prove myself, especially those who said that I would never perform well academically. So I enrolled in grad school, and I did better than I thought I would, graduating with a Master's Degree in Teaching with a 3.9 GPA. I had so many excuses to give up, but God wouldn't allow me to give up. He saw something else in me that I didn't see in myself, something that made me want to continue pressing and not give up, despite all the hurdles I had to jump over.

Even though I have a learning difference, I didn't allow it to interfere with my plans. What I had to realize, and you should too, is that good things never come easily. My difficulty was managing my disability and permitting it to stop me in my tracks; you need a way to push through. Learn and understand what it is that's genuinely demotivating you. Adjust your mindset, learn to deal with challenges, and you'll come out on the other side, a healthy and prosperous person.

CHAPTER 14

FALLING IN LOVE
WITH HIM AGAIN

When you fall in love with someone, that person may occupy your attention and all your time, or you can't help talking about him or her. You get up and go to sleep and think about the relationship and what the future may look like together. You feel secure, and you feel comfortable, appreciated, optimistic, and always content, and these are just a few positive emotions that you might feel. These were my feelings when I fell back in love with God.

At one point in my life, I wasn't in love with God the way I am now. I was too busy living my life, and not the one that God intended me to live. What I didn't realize was that I couldn't do what I wanted to do and still love God; it just wasn't working. My behaviors did not align with Christ at all. I was still having premarital sex, did what I wanted to do because I did not want to follow the plan God had for my life. I continued to have friendships with people who did not have a relationship with Christ and did not respect my religious values. I began to shift my relationship with Christ by having these things in my life or allowing them to surround me. All these things questioned my morals and faith in Christ, which are huge red flags that I ignored for a very long time just so I could feel loved, consistently happy, free, hopeful, and valued. God made me realize that I readily had all of these things when my relationship was steady with Him.

After realizing that this was going on, I had to do some soul-searching to see what had led me astray in the first place, so I unraveled my life to get to the root of the problem. What I found out was that I struggle with relationships, not just with men, but with everyone who has hurt me, including myself. I was hurt, and I wanted to be cherished and find love, too, but I was disappointed by most, if not all, of those who assured me they did.

Then I understood that my previous sins and shortcomings moved me farther apart from God, which rendered me isolated by my weight of shame and embarrassment. I had to be vulnerable and uncomfortable with myself, and I had to have the courage to face all my emotions, hurt, pain, and brokenness to get to the place I wanted to be in Christ. I had to give up control over all the aspects of my life that I had controlled for almost 20 years to finally experience God's grace.

Once I released control and allowed God to control every aspect of my life, I fell in love with God again; I felt the peace and happiness in my life that I hadn't felt in years. I felt protected; His voice was soft and clear, and I realized I wasn't alone. He assured me that He was with me, and I was with Him. I was hopeful, and I had the confidence to know God 's promise to me that He would always be with me, that He would protect me, that He would be my strength, that He would answer me, that He would give me peace, and that He would always love me.

Falling back in love with God has had its ups and downs, its bumps and its bruises, but I needed to go through it to know that it was the same love that He already had for me, and I was the only one who stopped loving Him; He never stopped loving me. I had to fall back in love with myself so that I could love God and realize that my life is not mine; it belongs to God. I had to realign myself with Christ and that meant, things I used to do I couldn't do any longer. I needed to surround myself with people who are on the same path as myself and put Christ first in their lives. I don't have to question my values or morals and my faith in Christ because now I know where I stand with Him, and He knows where I stand with him, and now I can say I'm genuinely in love with God now.

CHAPTER 15

THE DAY THINGS CHANGED

An unknown writer said, "If you do not create change, change will create you." We're often opposed to change because it's uncomfortable, or you might be afraid to leave your routine or familiar atmosphere. But with a transition, there is development, and without progress, you exist with no purpose. For me, adjusting to change has had its challenges. I only made moves toward the unknown if I believed and felt that the risks of standing still were higher than those shifting forward in a completely different direction, especially if it's unexpected. It's those unforeseen events that shake your world and invite or force us to interact with life in new ways.

It was 2017, and I worked as an instructional support specialist, and it was the end of my fourth year in this position. I wanted to do something different from what I was doing, so I looked at other opportunities like teaching. The chance to teach full-time had come, and I took advantage of the new opportunity. I was overly excited to finally have my classroom and work with the kids the way I wanted to. With this position came great responsibility and very overwhelming concern that I had little or no control over, but somehow it became my responsibility.

What I didn't realize was being a teacher would take over my life. I brought home my work and all the problems of that day. I would leave work and go back home and cry to my mom because some of my kids couldn't read, and they were in the sixth grade. I complained about the lack of resources the district had provided for my students with the unique needs they required. I also received a letter from a parent threatening my life, which the district ignored and did not take seriously. This transition wasn't going in the direction I thought it should be. Since it was my first year of teaching and getting my classroom, I figured it would be special. However, it brought little joy and happy memories. Still, it also carried with it a lot of fear, heartache, and confusion regarding my job in the field of education and what was about to happen next.

As my school year was about to end, I finally started to see the light at the end of the tunnel, and I was so happy to see it. I had plans to travel, relax, and live my life, but God changed my plans and quickly changed my life. It was May 2, 2018; I had called my mother on my lunch break just to talk to her and to see how she was doing. I told her I would call her back when I got off because my break was over, and I needed to get back to my class. Once I got off work and settled down, I called her back. I called her, but she didn't pick up the phone, so I called back a couple of minutes later, except this time, my nephew picked up and told me she was going to the hospital. I thought that something had happened to my brother, but he said that something was wrong with my mother. I was curious; I'd talked to her a couple of hours earlier, and she seemed fine. Then I called my brother, and he told me that the doctors were checking, but they figured she'd had a stroke. By this time, my heart was racing, and my mind was blank, because I was in shock, and I was trying to process what my brother had told me. I had to gather my thoughts, so I could call my family and tell them what was going on with my mom. I didn't know all the details, but I could only tell them what my brother had told me. And the only way I could know for sure was to fly out to Arizona, so I booked a flight for my son and myself, and we were in there the next day.

I arrived in Arizona early the next morning and went directly to the hospital to check on my mother. The doctors told me that she had suffered two strokes, had left side weakness, and slurred speech. She was responsive, and the next couple of days were going to be critical for her. Now things have certainly changed, not only for me but for my mother. She'd gone from being self-sufficient and independent to now having to be cared for and unable to walk, not over time, but in less than 24 hours. Over the next few days, I had to figure out what I was going to do and how my siblings and I were going to take care of my mother and what was best for her.

This sudden shift was dramatic, challenging, and uncomfortable, but I learned that immediate change is a normal part of life; nothing lasts forever. This unexpected change was so uncomfortable, and it threw my life off balance. I had to make the tough decision to walk away from my classroom and students six weeks before school was over. This was necessary in order to travel back and forth to Arizona as I prepared for my mom to move back to California to live with me. I left my son with family friends, which was painful to do because He had school projects that I needed and wanted to be there for. For the first time in my son's life, I missed a parent-teacher conference, his year-end performance and award ceremony, and that hurt like hell.

When we returned to Oakland, my life changed even further. My mom lived with me now, and my personal space and privacy were no longer available. I gave my mom my bedroom, and I took over the living room, so that's where I slept. I had to cook and clean, run all my mom's errands, including mine, and I took her to her doctor's appointments. My sister and I took turns bathing and other things, which helped out a lot, but this new routine and the sudden transition were not as easy as everyone assumed; I just made it appear that way. I no longer had a personal life; all my plans for the summer were no more. Dating was out of the picture because it was so time-consuming, and I wasn't in the right frame of mind to do it either. I didn't even have time to hang out with my friends, and if I did, it would just be for a couple of hours, and nothing more because I had to take care of my mom.

These changes were beneficial because they forced me to grow emotionally, physically, and depend more on God. I could no longer live the same, and it forced me to think differently about the events and circumstances of my life. It even forced me to reconsider my values and priorities for my life. This change meant a new beginning, and with fresh starts, other things must come to an end. It forced me to reconsider the choices and decisions I had made to that point. My life was never going to be the same, and I needed to embrace it.

This transition helped me develop resilience and regain the strength of character I'd lost over the years. It pushed me into awkward and challenging circumstances that motivated me to demonstrate the confidence I required to move on. Changing for the better is what can keep you empowered and encouraged on your new path. Surround yourself with individuals who have achieved significant improvements in their lives and ask them all sorts of questions regarding their progress. Still, you have to assume complete accountability for the adjustments you'd like to create in your life because if you don't, you will continue to see no progress in your life.

CHAPTER 16

THE LOVES I LOST

Losing someone can bring a lot of emotions, and it can be overwhelming. Some deaths are unexpected, and some deaths you have months to prepare for, but even if you have months to prepare for their passing, it still brings shock, disbelief, anger, and deep sadness. I lost two people in 2019 who I loved deeply: one was an ex-boyfriend whose death was sudden, and the other was my sister, whose death I was preparing for, but nothing prepared me.

January 7, 2019, is a day that I can never forget. I had just come back from a doctor's visit, so I was in a good place when I received a phone call asking me to check my social media page; my ex-boyfriend may have passed away. I reached out to his relatives, and they confirmed that he had died. I was shocked, and I felt it was unbelievable. I sat in my car for an hour and cried before I went into my house to tell my mom and my son that he had passed away. After I told them, I went to my bathroom, broke down and cried for two hours. That night, I cried myself to sleep, I wished that all this was just a dream, that I would wake up the next day, and it wouldn't be real, but it was.

His death hit me hard because we were still friends after we broke up. He'd always check on my son and me, or he'd cut my son's hair if I needed his hair cut, or we'd see each other if I went to my family home. He also showed up at my grandmother's funeral to show some support, love, and respect. We just had that kind of connection after we broke up where we respected each other's relationship and never created a problem.

He messaged me out of the blue three months before he passed away, and we messaged each other for more than an hour, catching up and reminiscing about old times. Once he reached out, we kept in touch with each other, and we'd chat for hours a few days, or we'd check on each other to see how each other's day was going on. He didn't sound the same; he sounded mature and seemed happy with his life, and I complimented him on how mature he sounded.

His last text message to me was "Merry Christmas," and I told him I would see him when I got back from Chicago, but that day would never come. His death hit me hard for so many reasons. He was my first love; he was a father to my son for the first four years of his life, he loved me for me and accepted all my flaws. He never judged me, and he allowed me to be myself. His love was genuine and like no other. He was more than a boyfriend, he was my friend, and it showed, but most of all, he was a true man, and you couldn't take that from him. He will forever have a piece of my heart, and I will always love L.R.S. Rest in Love.

My sister's death was the second death that I experienced within two months, and it hurt my family and the people who loved and cared for her hard. We all knew that her time was limited, but nothing could prepare us for March 17, 2019. I was in church when my nephew called and told me that she had passed away. I was devastated because I had spoken to her the day before, and she assured me that she was doing all right, and she asked if Jaylen and I were going to her house on Sunday, and I told her yes.

When I was 11 or 12 years old, I met her. She and my brother dated in high school and married shortly after that. She moved to our home when she was pregnant with my nephew while my brother went to (Marine) Boot-camp. That's when our relationship started, and she quickly became my sister. She stayed with us a little while before she moved to 29 Palms Ca because that's where my brother was stationed. Once they settled down in their place, I stayed with them for a summer, and we would watch movies, laugh, play cards, and talk. She moved back to Oakland and into our home because she and my brother had some problems, and she and my nephews would stay with us until she got her place. Even though she and my brother had broken off their relationship, she still remained my sister.

Our sistership lasted 28 years, and it was just that. We had our disagreements like any sibling relationship, and we would make up. I was there when she gave birth to both of my nephews and helped name one of them. We had our unique way of greeting each other, which was "L for love" and "L" meant "Loser," but deep down, it meant "L for Love." She was a warrior in every aspect of her life and never gave up until she had reached the ambitions she set for herself. She struggled with a lot of diseases that almost took her out, but she was resilient, and she overcame the matter shining.

My sister's health started to worsen in January 2019. I just got off work, and I had a couple of missed calls and texts, telling me to go to the hospital to check on my sister. I called my nephew to see what was going on, and he said that I should go up to the hospital. I finally arrived, and my sister was not doing well. They had her attached to so many machines, and tubes were everywhere. The doctors took my nephew and me to another section of the waiting room and informed us to get in touch with all the family and advise them to get to the hospital because she may not make it. I called my other sister and my sister's friends and told them to come to the hospital soon since she might not make it through the night. The first night was scary because we didn't realize what was going to happen. We hadn't noticed any changes for nearly three days, and suddenly things began to turn around for her.

She spent several days in ICU before they moved her to a different floor of the hospital. Her cancer had returned and spread to her lungs and spine, and the doctors had a meeting with the family, telling us that there was nothing else they could do, and they were going to send her home on hospice, and they would make her as comfortable as possible. We were still hopeful during this process and prayed that things would change. Family and friends would take turns caring for her and spending as much time as we could until March 17, 2019, when God wanted her to be in His presence. Rest Well, Michelle, L for Love.

CHAPTER 17

LISTENING TO THE VOICE

Listening can be simple for some and difficult for others; listening will either preserve your life or kill you. Listening involves giving someone your attention and noticing what someone says. Either you respond to the advice, or it's a request and make an effort to do what someone says. Either way, you have a choice to listen, or you don't. With listening comes understanding intimacy, inspiration, and persuasion. What it can bring is health, well-being, and you can learn, but listening to the right voice can change your life, or your life can be adjusted for you.

As you can see, my life has been far from perfect, and the only way I could begin to see a difference was to make lifestyle changes, which required surrendering to Christ. This meant that I had to yield total control of every part of my life, allowing God to be the head and be willing to listen to Him. Doing so is not a straightforward process, particularly if you have never given all your life to Christ before. Surrendering may be frustrating and unpleasant, but it was vital for me to do so, and if I didn't do that, I realized I was not making a lifestyle change, nor was I listening.

God has His ways to get you to listen to him, and he got me to do just that. I recall the night that I clearly heard the voice of God. I was crying because my life was all over the place, and I was sick of things being that way, and I decided to give up on my life because my life had given up on me. There was a still, small voice that said, "I realize you 're exhausted, and I realize you want to give up on life, but if you just give me a chance to let me show you the way, I got you." I glanced around my bedroom, and there wasn't anyone, but I sensed a spirit right next to me, and I fell asleep. It was the first time in months that I slept through the night, and that morning, I woke up rejuvenated, feeling like a new individual.

After hearing God's voice, my life began to shift, but to continue hearing His word, I needed to adjust my way of thinking. I had to change my attitude from wanting to do what I wanted to do to do what God wanted me to do. I had to break the obstacles of pride, fear, and bitterness that stopped me from hearing God's voice. The pride I was having was that I could handle anything and try Him when life got too rough. This behavior prevented me from recognizing the voice of God distinctly and stopped my development in Christ. The fear was that God would have full control of my life, and doing what he wanted me to do was scary, and hearing voices might have you thinking like you're going crazy, and I didn't want that. One thing I wanted to get rid of was the bitterness in my heart. I needed to give up my right to be angry at anyone who had hurt me or been upset with for years. That bitterness stopped me from recognizing Him plainly and blocked my blessings. I couldn't go to God to beg Him to forgive me and hear my prayer if I didn't do the same thing.

After removing fear, pride, and bitterness, my relationship with Christ became a little more intimate, his presence had become apparent, and there were a couple of things I had to keep in mind. When I hear God's voice, is that something I hear contradicting or supporting what the Scripture says? Is what I hear representing the character of God? Will it bear the fruit of the spirit? Lastly, does what I hear bring hope and peace from God?

I had to make myself open to listening, which meant that I had to set aside time to be in God's presence by praying, meditating on his word, or writing in my journal. I also had to be willing to obey what he asked me to do, even if it sounded insane. By not doing these things, I will disobey Him, putting a rift between God and me, and the further you get from God, the harder it becomes to hear Him. Through hearing God's voice clearly, my life has changed so much that I have peace and happiness, and I recognize his voice as he talks to me, so I am no longer scared, nor do I question where I stand in Christ.

CHAPTER 18

CHANGING THE NARRATIVE & BREAKING THE CYCLE

Have you ever noticed a destructive trend in your life that occurs much too often? Too many times to be a coincidence? You're beginning to realize that you've experienced this before, but you continue doing the same thing, producing the same outcomes. The same behavior persists until you decide enough is enough, so you end the cycle that you've been on for years. Many may call this a life cycle and I had been here for almost 20 years; it was time to end it.

I was just a young girl, wanting to be accepted by someone and didn't know how to convey it, so I expressed it in ways that would confuse my life. I saw things at a young age that you weren't supposed to see, like people having sex and wondering how it felt — never having the "sex talk" was just being told not to do it. I was curious, and I found out on my own; I didn't know I'd be exploring a whole new world that would change my life forever. This lifestyle became mine at a very early age, and I didn't slow down until later in my life. What I had to experience at this time in my life is something no kid should.

I noticed my body being admired and stared at by older men, and how ashamed and awkward it made me feel at that young age. What I discovered was that occasionally I could get what I wanted. What I didn't think, though, and would figure out later in life, is that it would mess me up mentally and emotionally and create an unhealthy lifestyle. I was unlearning to love and value myself, never establishing boundaries for anyone in my life, and not standing up when others violated them. I didn't respect myself or love myself. I didn't have someone to hold me accountable for my actions, nor did I think or feel that I was doing anything wrong. So I continued this lifestyle in secret and shame until one day, my eyes opened, and I knew that the way of life I practiced was no longer a productive lifestyle for me. I was able to confront the suffering I had been going through for much of my life that I caused.

I was in my late thirties when I realized that I was repeating the same cycle over again. It was the same lifestyle, such as dating the same type of guys and doing the same thing year after year, producing the same results, unhappy, heartbroken, lost, and not loving myself. I was never in peace, and I was tired, but I was determined to break the cycle this time. I had to figure out why I had continued the same behavior pattern. What I found out was I had never dealt with past issues like breakups, verbal and emotional abuse, relational issues, and other things. The only way to break the cycle was to get help to get to the root of the problem, so I reached out for help.

Life had been so much; I had just ended my four-year relationship, my mom had a stroke, my sister's health was declining, and I was struggling with anxiety; I was drained. I was exhausted, thinking that I had it all together and that I was okay, so I reached out to my doctor.

My doctor recognized that I wasn't alright and realized that my issues were the source of my anxiety. She directed me to a therapist to get to the heart of the question. I also asked my pastor for spiritual guidance because I needed help to address specific problems in my life centered around my Christian beliefs.

The step to seek help is where I had to begin because I didn't want to continue down the path that caused me so much pain. I realize that I'd created most of the chaos by allowing others to treat me in a manner that wasn't loving or respectful, and I deserved this type of treatment. This chaos in my life caused the anxiety, and the only way to deal with it was to face it head-on and all the emotions.

First of all, I had to realize that I had to change my behavior and hold myself responsible. I needed to learn to love and value myself, establish limits with others in my life and speak up when people ignored them. I needed to surround myself with people who would hold me responsible for my decisions and challenge me anytime they saw me out of my character. I also learned to use the tools I learned in therapy, take one day at a time, and not to be too hard on myself. Eventually, I needed to realize that God's mercy was an essential aspect of my healing, and was the only way to break the chains and continue in the right direction.

When I did all of this, I began to see the cycle and the repeated dysfunctional behavior. Going through this was not easy to do. I had to reflect on all the pain and negative perceptions that were causing me to act out. I learned to love, respect, and value myself and find peace within me. I had to surround myself with others who would hold me accountable for my actions and keep me in check. I had to change the narrative that I created about myself and break the cycle. I couldn't continue this lifestyle in secret and shame because I don't want anyone to repeat a harmful lifestyle that I experienced. By telling my story, I can help others break the patterns and generational curses leading them down the wrong path and find their peace and happiness in a new lifestyle.

CHAPTER 19

THE BIG MOVE

Moving to a new state can be a life-changing and overwhelming thing to do, especially if you have lived in one place all your life as I did. Oakland had become too stressful for me, and the cost of living had increased. Oakland's leadership did not appear to care, and the crime rate was becoming higher, and gentrification had become real. The place I'd been calling home my entire life didn't seem like home anymore. I began to feel trapped, and I was missing out on my life, so I wanted a new start, but where am I going to move?

I had a couple of locations in mind, like Iowa, North Carolina, Arizona, and Texas. I'd considered looking at Iowa because there was a college there that was the perfect match for my son, but I couldn't do it because of the weather, I couldn't do the snow in the winter. I also couldn't be that far from my family, and I didn't know anyone out there. Then there was North Carolina. I had a couple of friends who moved there, and they spoke about how beautiful it was and how inexpensive the cost of living was. Again, I didn't want to be too far away from my family, and I didn't think it would remind me of my home, and I needed that. I began looking at Arizona, too, as it was close to my mom. She had already suffered a stroke, so I figured it would be smart to stay next to her. The cost of living was not high; the climate was pleasant, but there was little diversity, and the salary for a teacher was not impressive at all. The last place I was thinking of moving to was Texas. A good friend of mine had just moved in and spoke about how beautiful it was, how pleasant the weather was, and how inexpensive the cost of living was. I went to see that it was everything she had mentioned, and I fell in love with Texas.

After coming back from my visit to Houston, I started doing my research. I began looking at the cost of living and whether it was affordable compared to where I was staying. Then I looked at roles in my career, and whether my income would be the same as in California. Next, I looked at the community and the area that I decided to stay in, and it seemed pretty safe and quiet. I searched for colleges for my son and whether they had his major and how close they were to where we were moving. Another thing I was hoping for was if this place would bring me peace and happiness?

After doing my research, I found out the cost of living and houses was lovely. There was a significant disparity; I could buy two houses in Texas for the price of my home in Oakland. I noticed the salary for positions in my career was almost better than in California, and I didn't have to live to work, I could work and live. The community I looked at was relatively new and safe, and I didn't have to go outside of the city I lived in for shopping at all, unlike what I had to do in Oakland. For my son, the college he considered going to was an hour away, and if he was considering going to a community college, there was one in the neighborhood I was looking to move. Lastly, I went to visit Texas four different times to see if I felt the same way as I did when I first visited, and it was the same every time.

After my last visit to Texas, I could see how affordable it was and how wiser it was for me to move than to stay in California, so I made plans to fix up my home and put it on the market for sale. I told my family and friends, some were supportive of the move, and some were not so supportive. I could no longer care what others thought of the choices I was making because they didn't have to live my life, I did.

I wanted more in my life for myself and my son, so to do that, I had to move. Our last year in Oakland was a stressful one. I started having anxiety attacks in my own house more often because of all the noise in my neighborhood that never stopped. My son and I had three deaths less than three months apart, and we were ready to move. I knew in my heart that it was time to leave and I had made the right choice to move. Now, all I had to do was trust God because that's all I had left.

Some may think I was selfish to move to another state, but that's not true. This move was all God's doing. He was the one who put this place in my heart, and I had the option to listen to His voice, or I could ignore Him. I've been doing things my way for years now, and it was time to depend on God and do what he wanted me to do, not what I wanted to do. This change has been life-changing, and so far, it's been fantastic. I don't feel anxious now, nor have I experienced an anxiety attack in quite a long time. I feel safe and secure, and I don't feel stuck or unhappy in my life.

Finally, don't feel obligated to live in a place where the cost of living is too high, and you're struggling financially every month. It's all right to walk on from the place you've been calling home all your life for a fresh start in a different, unfamiliar place that could be what you need. Never let anyone deter you from taking steps that can save your life and liberate you from what's held you back.

CITED

Hudson, R. F., High, L., & Otaiba, S. A. (n.d.). Dyslexia and the Brain: What Does Current Research Tell Us? Retrieved June 4, 2020, from http://www.ldonline.org/article/14907/

CHAPTER 20

JUST WAIT ON GOD CAUSE IT'S NOT WORTH IT

Staying where you are, or delaying action for a given moment, or until something significant occurs, is described as waiting, which some of us may have a hard time doing, and it is something that I struggled with over the years. I have learned that speeding things up for your life may be a form of suicide. We often place a time limit for ourselves to get a house, your dream job, getting married, or having children. But what some of us don't understand is that our timing isn't the same as God's. His plans don't require our permission, and they don't operate on our timetable. When we want to hurry up the natural rate of life, it may be to our disadvantage. By not waiting, we can cause suffering to ourselves and others, or your blessings could be blocked or even denied, you will not be in the will of God.

If I had a dollar for every time I should have waited on

God, I'd be a millionaire, and I wouldn't be writing a chapter telling you to wait on him either. But instead, I am writing a chapter to ask you to wait on Him because it's not worth it. I believe the moments that I decided not to wait altered the course of my life. Like waiting to have sex until I got married, or having a child out of wedlock and waiting for God to send me the person who was just for me. This way of thinking landed me in a lot of trouble on more than one occasion.

I knowingly didn't wait because I wanted to do what I wanted to do. And what I purposely ignored and failed to realize was that waiting is a vital aspect of Christian life because, as I have discovered, there are significant consequences for not using this spiritual discipline. I was out of God's will when I made the decision to have sex before marriage, when I had my child out of wedlock, and when I didn't wait for Him. With God, you can't have your cake and eat it too because the moment you go ahead of God is the moment you step out of His will.

Quick decisions and impulsive behavior can be justified for a child, but not so much for experienced Christians. As a Christian, I knew better, but I allowed outside influences to change my thoughts and behavior to do the complete opposite. So, because of my immaturity, I'm pretty sure I was blocking myself from receiving blessings. God is more concerned with your maturity in Christ than with your blessings and will withhold blessings until you mature and learn from your mistakes.

At some point in life, you have to learn to wait. Waiting can be beneficial to your life, especially if you're a Christian. Waiting on God is a crucial part of your relationship with Christ. It says that you trust Him even when you don't know what His plan is, and it establishes a more profound love for you, and when God loves, He loves.

CONCLUSION

I shared my last 20 years with you because I wanted to shed some light on my life and share the things I've gone through. At first, I was reluctant to share what I experienced because I was ashamed and embarrassed about all the things I had gone through. It was important that I no longer silence myself or suppress my opinions, ideas, and experiences; I wanted to help those who might be looking for a change and encourage them to change. I also wanted to show that we can learn from every experience we have in life, good or bad. I know that life still has lessons to teach me and I am open to moving ahead in life with faith and love.

This book wasn't just for me; it was for those who see themselves repeating the same patterns that have proved to not serve them in the past. This book is for those who don't want to repeat the same life cycle as their loved ones and want and need to break the cycle that is producing the same results. It's for the person that has yet to believe in their own self-worth. It's for the person who's been in abusive relationships and doesn't know how to seek help or leave. It's for those who are starting to realize we need self-love before we can seek love from others. It's for those who are facing challenges they don't believe they can overcome. And finally, it's for the person who said enough is enough, but is still uncertain about the next steps and is looking for support.

I hope this book proves that your life matters, what you've done, or what has been done to you does not have to define and control you. Most importantly you don't have to sit and be silent anymore and do it alone. I encourage you to succeed in everything you do, make a positive impact on the lives of others, and love God on purpose.